Poetic Recovery

Sandra Gould

Published by New Generation Publishing in 2018

Copyright © Sandra Gould 2018

First Edition

The author asserts the moral right under the Copyright, Designs and Patents Act 1988 to be identified as the author of this work.

All Rights reserved. No part of this publication may be reproduced, stored in a retrieval system or transmitted, in any form or by any means without the prior consent of the author, nor be otherwise circulated in any form of binding or cover other than that in which it is published and without a similar condition being imposed on the subsequent purchaser.

www.newgeneration-publishing.com

Friend

A good friend is what you've been
I've poured out my heart, it's all been seen
You've been patient and listened to me cry
I need to start living again, at least give it a try
I've caused you stress and I'm sorry for that
at times you must of felt like a door mat
I feel stronger and at peace tonight
In my head it's like, on goes the light
I will start afresh and move away
thank you again for having your say
You are one of the best friends ever
and that friendship will never sever
I'll live near the beach, and be in the sun all day
just a few hours working if I may
Thank you for everything you have done for me
you need to slow down, of that I can see
You work long hours, and drive here and there
look after your health, after all I do care

Dawlish

Dawlish is the place I want to be
I'll be so happy with my family around me
I lay in the sun and get a golden tan
this is for me, not any man
I watch the waves, beat and crash
at certain times, up it will lash
The turn of the tide, to watch is such fun
and it changes again when out comes the sun
The seagulls wait for scraps of food
seeing them will change my mood
people are dozing in their deckchairs
while others go up and down selling their wares
I lay on the beach and start to dream
Is my life all what it seems?
So much has happened in the last year
but for now I have my family near

The Beach

Down on the beach I'm happy and free
looking out, as far as you can see
No one can hurt me, I'm far away
the pain is still with me, most of the day
My broken heart needs to repair
walking on the sand, I don't have a care
I close my eyes and imagine your kiss
If things could of been different, I only wish
I will stay alone now and avoid the pain
there is much in that to be gained
I'll walk on the beach, but to myself I will keep
while no ones around I'll softly weep
Men and friends are in my past
that is something that will ever last
On my own I will always be
come and find me, and you will see
Existing is now what I'll do with my life
I remember twice when i was a wife
The person that I am is so very bad
but the pain I'm feeling makes me so sad
I want to go to sleep and never wake
this is my plan for me to make

Rehab

Alcoholic and drug addicts fill the centre
they leave behind their family as they enter
They have a buddy who shows them around
some come in and don't utter a sound
Some come in drunk, while others are high
but most of them won't even look you in the eye
Some have been injecting and some popping pills
they start their detox and begins the chills
Their nose starts to run and they start to shake
some find the detox too much, and they break
Many relapse and come back again
it's hard to stay clean and break that chain
Some unfortunately don't make it and die
we all ask that same question, why?
Some people crave drink and some drugs
while ignorant people think they are mugs
Nobody chooses to be an addict
perhaps they're the ones who have been handpicked
It's an illness and they can't help being that way
let's hope more like me aren't afraid to say

Death

The thought of death doesn't scare me
my cat will be waiting for me to see
No more hurt, no more pain
surely there must be something to be gained
Life is cruel and sometimes hard
I'll write my feelings down in a card
My life has come to an all too quick end
the pain I'm feeling can never mend
I'm going somewhere very soon
and I'll be watching you from the moon
play George Michael and think of me
he's up there singing, I can't wait to see.

Rain

The skies are grey and down comes the rain
It's not very long until it fills the drain
Children jump in the puddles and laugh and scream
they play for hours or so it seems
Sometimes it rains and the sun comes out
there's a rainbow, the children shout
The fine drizzle is what I really dislike
seeing people soaked, while riding their bikes
Sometimes you can't keep an umbrella up, as the wind is so strong
when it's heavy, stay in, all day long
When it rains, it gets us down
looking for shops to shelter in the town
Everything now is soaking wet
there's washing on the line, the women fret
Another day, and it's wet again
wrong again, is my weather vane
It's tipping it down now, but it's good for the plants
moan about rain again, no I shan't

A Child

A child is the most precious gift
holding them close to you, gives you a lift
Will it be a girl or will it be a boy?
whatever it is, will bring much joy
You nurture the baby and hold it tight
some of us, watch them throughout the night
A miracle is the only way to describe a baby
would you do it again? maybe
That rush of love when it's placed in your arms,
you lay there at peace and so calm
You hold the baby and look so happy
but all too soon and it's time to change the nappy
Bursting with pride are the new mum and dad
looking in I can see blue, and see they have a little lad

The Forest

The forest is deep with so many trees
they go on for miles as far as you can see
100's of years some have been here
some look scary as I stand and stare
Some trees are small and some are tall
try and climb them and you would fall
The forest is dense and very thick
at times I think I'm lost and feel very sick
Horses, cows and donkeys roam free
pass them by, and leave them be
Tadpoles swim freely in the streams
then a snake, or an eel, or so it seems
Dogs run about and bark for their master
they bark and bark as they run much faster
In the distance sometimes you will see a deer
watch for a while, then go for a beer

Football

Football is a game of two teams
to win a cup, is what they dream
Scoring goals is the aim of the game
some weeks we watch the goalkeeper take all the blame
The referees decision can alter the game
while the crowd start jeering and calling him names
The linesman has to be on the ball
if not, it could end in a brawl
A goal has been scored, and the crowd start to cheer
the away end aren't happy and begin to jeer
Someone's been fouled and the ref gives a penalty
the strikers stand in front of the goal, like it's his destiny
The goal goes in and the crowd celebrate
was it a penalty, that's cause for a debate
The crowd start to leave, jeering on the way out
their not happy they lost, there's no doubt
Next week, we will all be back again
praying for a win, and probably sat in the rain

TV

At night I sit and watch the soaps
to live their lives, we sometimes hope
They never work and sit about in the pub all day
living that way, just wouldn't pay
We love the arguments and the fights
and relive them long into the night
We view the actors as our family and friends
and the ones we like best, we always defend
Weddings, babies and deaths, we have it all on there
we watch it all, without a care
Eastenders is so depressing it sucks
all of the residents are down on their luck
Murder, bed hopping it all goes on
to be part of the cast, we sometimes long
They never mention football on the soaps
it's more about kids running off to elope
Reality TV is a must for me
can't believe these actors get paid a fee
has been celebs think they're all that on set
and on certain shows, we laugh when they get wet
Our telly is watched for many hours a day
and whatever is on, we somehow pay

Mental Health

Mental health is at an all time high
ask the medical professionals and they'd probably lie
OCD, PTSD, depression and panic attacks are things we hear everyday
Social anxiety, I'll learn about along the way
Cannabis has a lot to answer for
youngsters today smoke it more and more
They think they feel good as it alters their mind
I try to tell them this, although I'm only being kind
It scares me how big mental health has got
medical teams put it all under one umbrella, the whole bloody lot
People are on the streets, many causing harm
they need help and medication to keep them calm
Eradicate the drugs and the problems might ease
a drug free country, wouldn't that please
If it carries on now as it has been
many of the youngsters will die and I'm not being mean
The government needs to spend out on mental health
we have all at some stage suffered, just look at yourself
Go into schools championing the word, make it a date
act now before it's too late

My Cat

Sooty was my beautiful cat
I loved her so, you can be sure of that
My world was over the day she died
I sat indoors and cried and cried
Around my neck, I wear her fur
I close my eyes and hear her purr
loyal to me, of that you can be sure
I wanted her with me, forever more
Her fur was so soft to touch
she made me happy, so very much
Daily I think of her, and yes I still miss
especially when she used to give me a kiss
Wherever I go, she is with me
one day we'll be reunited, you'll see

Summer's Coming

The summer season is almost here
people coming in the shop full of beer
People are red where they've been out in the sun
kids running about having fun
People are laughing, splashing about in the sea
while others are in there, only up to their knees
People sit about eating fish and chips
while some go out and about on day trips
Children playing ball and some with kites
I try to watch them, but the sun is too bright
Some people find it too hot, so they sit in the shade
on the beach it's a mass of buckets and spades
Not long now and the nights will start to draw in
and I'll sit back and think, what a good summer it's been

Politics

Tories or Labour, who do I choose
of them all someone will loose
out of their mouths, the lies that they tell
thinking they will trap us with their cheap sale
fox hunting is back says Theresa May
are you that stupid? It never went away
Jeremy Corbin promises a reckoning for tax cheats
and brexit could be hijacked by the wealthy elite
Thatcher, Kinnock, Blair and Major are all gone, but in our past
we need someone young, strong and new to last
The BBC has been accused of breach by the greens
they all act like children and behave so mean
I'm undecided if I will vote
I'd rather spend the day in a boat
Politics in this country is all a sham
as 1 out of 3 of us don't give a dam

Me

I look in the mirror and feel so old
each winter now, I feel the cold
I'm fast approaching 50 and feel so sad
I want to act reckless and be bad
I'm old and single, what a mess
ask me how I feel, and I might express
I have a heart condition, which doesn't scare me
but I'm a tough cookie, just leave me be
There's lines on my face and grey in my hair
mention it, you wouldn't dare
I've had ¾ of my life
for over half of it, I was a wife
What is 50? A number some say
I'll take a year off on my next birthday

Work

Life is hard, all we do is work
some are workshy and will often shirk
We spend each day there, all day long
some might say, this is wrong
Some have good jobs, some have bad
some make us happy, while some make us sad
Work is where most of our life is spent
this is the way that it is meant
Some of us work for the minimum wage
while others work past their retirement age
Some jobs you have to train for
and other jobs do nothing but bore
A job is now called your career
we all want to work by home, and so near
Our friends are often our workmates
and some even go out on dates
The end of the month is when we get paid
if your company's in the red, it may be delayed

So Low

Today I want to stay in bed and shut out the world
pull the duvet over me, and lay there curled
Everything looks black and grey today
wish I could just take off and run away
I go to the kitchen and pop a pill
does it help? It never will
depression is the word for how I feel
me depressed, it's so unreal
I've lost my confidence and my memory is poor
feeling like this, there must be a cure
I look in the mirror and feel ugly and so fat
God help me please, I feel so flat
some days I get up and my mood is so low
how did I get here? That I don't know
There are thousands of people out there like me
I want it to go, so I can be free
I don't have feelings, I just feel numb
I have to be strong, to overcome
My head is a mess and needs to repair
why am I like this? It isn't fair

Ian Brady

So at long last, Ian Brady is dead
although god knows why he was being force fed
His crimes shocked the nation
and he was placed incarceration
Why is it the main news today?
he should of been killed years ago, what was the delay?
He showed no remorse for the crimes he did
and he never spoke about the bodies he hid
What makes someone behave so extreme?
Although him and Hindley must of schemed
Are there anymore we don't know about?
of that I very much doubt
He has taken his crimes with him to hell
where the bodies were buried, he never did tell
Psychopath, mental or evil, what is he?
the good thing is, he never walked free
Keeping him in prison has cost thousands of pounds
the parents of the victims have made not a sound
They've behaved with dignity, despite what he did to their child
there's no sorrow for you, for those children that you defiled
You're an evil man, who I don't want to read about
burn in hell and suffer as you bow out

Alcohol & Drugs

A massive problem is alcohol & drugs
most of us associate crime with thugs
these people need help and lots of care
when you see them on the street, stop and think, do not stare
Some have lost everything that they once had
some are mothers and even dads
They live on the streets, as they have nowhere else to go
we think we are better than them, we're not, even so
They drink and take drugs to pass the time
and most of the time it leads to crime
On the streets living, no one should be
the government should try it, I'd like to see
Sort out the drugs and the drink
there's got to be a way, sit and think
Build more houses and limit how many come in
tackle this now, or you're never win

Cancer

It all starts when you find a lump on your body
You phone the Dr, you need to talk to somebody
Bloods and tests are all done
You want results now, but there are none
You wait and you are given the news
You have several options that you can choose
Malignant is the word they use
This tumour in my body has been let loose
They grade it and check what stage it's at
I can't take it in; I sit still, while they still chat
The first round of chemo goes quite quick
But each round after, I'm violently sick
My hair has all gone, and I'm completely bald
I hate you cancer, or whatever you're called
Poison runs through my body, and, I feel so ill
Getting better? I feel I'm going downhill
I'm booked in for several rounds of radiation next
I can't even speak now, I sit there perplexed
It's 6 months since the treatment, and I'm in the clear
But each day I will remain in fear

Tattoos

1 in 3 people have them now
I look at some, and think oh wow
each of our tattoos are special to us
I had all of mine without any fuss
Some have them all over their face
while others are covered without any space
I have some flowers on my feet
I thinks it's tasteful and very neat
Some have them all over their hands
I want one on mine, that is one of my plans
Some tattoos are very colourful
the more detail, tattooist has to be careful
Mine are special to me
and if you ask, I might let you see

Dementia

So many of our elderly have now got dementia
one minute they know you, and the next it's mass hysteria
They forget the things they used to know
but remember things from long ago
Some you have to feed, just like a child
and some days, you look and they almost smiled
They are not the person they once were
their minds are fussy and often a blur
Dementia comes in different forms
for some families it is the norm
Each person will react to it, in their own way
problems with communicating, and can't have their say
They get confused and some have mood swings
some sit in their own little world, and sit and sing
More and more get diagnosed each year
we all pray we will stay in the clear
This disease is so cruel by far
it doesn't escape you, even if you're a star

Ice Cream

Ice cream or lolly? What do you pick
some choose a lolly which they can lick
Some have an ice cream with a flake
some have ice cream on top of a cheesecake
There's loads of different ice creams out there
some have double cones, that you can share
Vanilla is the flavour that I like the best
chocolate and coffee I very much detest
There are many ways that you can eat it
some even have it with a banana split
There's every colour of the rainbow
with sprinkles and chocolate or cookie dough
Where I work we mainly sell magnum
this is the perfect ice cream for some
Mini milk is a favourite with the kids
it would make life a lot easier if they came with lids
However you have it, ice cream is so nice
and all the flavours that try to entice

Me

I used to be confident happy and gay
now I'm broken and sad every day
I don't trust and don't think I ever will
I won't even accept going out for a meal
Men and fun are in my past
feeling like this, how long will it last
I've gone mad with tattoos, is it self harm
I get another one, and almost feel calm
I want a nice man to look after me
they ask me out and I say, I'll see
My heart has been broken and can never mend
I always say no, sorry if it offends
Men always hurt me, so I'll stay alone now
and that is something that I will vow
They lie and cheat and play with your mind
yet I've heard there are a few that are really so kind
I'll never be happy again with a man
will try again one day, if I can
For me now, it's far too late
I can't even see I'll get another date

Lottery

Tonight the lottery is a massive jackpot
will I win it, I think not
People are excited incase they win
me, I want to get married, not live in sin
So many tickets bought with their hard earned cash
some buy loads and act so flash
What would I do if the winner was me
I'd have my own funeral business, just you see
People have stories about what they would do
while others think and don't have a clue
You could change some lives if you won
I'd have a business and look after my loved ones
Would it change the person that you are
some go mad, buying this and acting a star
I would like to think it wouldn't change me
first I have to win it, and then, we'll see

Martin Luther King

Martin Luther King was born in 1929
even to this day, many flock to his shrine
He was an activist and an American Baptist
he knew his stuff and was well practised
He was only 39 years old when he died
when this happened the public cried and cried
In 1957 he was the first SCLC president
he was good at his job, that was evident
I have a dream was his famous speech
he wasn't one to openly preach
In 1964 he received a nobel peace prize
collecting this, you could see the tears in his eyes
In 1968 he was assassinated by James Earl Ray
at the time, everyone wanted him to pay
After his death, there were many riots
but all too soon, it died down and all was quiet
James Earl Ray was sentenced to 99 years
when the verdict was read, you could hear the cheers
Martin Luther King lives on to this day
he did some great things, think of him often if you may

Mum and Dad

50 years together that's you and dad
50 years with one person would drive me mad
With the same person, it's such a long time to be
there's plenty more, let's wait and see
Bingo with your mums, is where you met
people play now and get into debt
Myself and Paul are the children you had
it was good having a brother, something, I'm so very glad
You took us out and we had such fun
but our best days were on the beach in the sun
Our cousins came and we all used to play
wouldn't it be nice to turn back the clock for a day
We used to meet dad from work in that old van
all the kids used to get in, as many as we can
Mum didn't drive and walked everywhere
even when she got wet, she didn't care
You are now great grandparents, which has made you proud
and another one on the way, to announce, I'm now allowed
Your grandchildren love you, as different as they all are
yet it is only Paige who has a car
Thank you for all the love and support you have given me
I'm so much better now, watch and see
You really are the best mum and dad
and yes I'm so very glad
I love you both with all my heart
mum don't cry, I know you'll start
What an achievement is 50 years
soon you will both be a pair of old dears

Musicals

Musicals for me is my real passion
some like sport and some follow fashion
I love it when the actors start to sing
and a bit of romance, and the happiness it brings
The sound of music, for me is the best
I know all about this film, I would even take a test
I could watch this film all day, every day
no work, sat in all day watching, I could if I may
To watch a musical on a stage is so great
but it's even better, if you go while on a date
I'm not just in the audience, I'm part of the show
I know all the words and all the songs, yes I am in the know
I've seen many, but I think my favourite was the Jersey Boys
the singing was so good and the actors had so much poise
Mamma Mia is such a happy musical to see
most men won't watch, would rather flee
I don't go to watch live shows anymore
I don't think I'd like to go alone, I'm a bit unsure
I have no one to go with now
but I will find a theatre buddy, I will vow

Alcohol

Alcohol is the sin of all sins
I'm throwing all my bottles in the bin
You drink it first and it makes you feel good
I want to feel like this all the time if I could
It poisons your body and fizzles your brain
alcohol is nothing but a pain
My head is a mess, remembering what did I do
did I do this, did I do that, I haven't a clue
You forget what you did and are so sad
a life like this, you must be mad
Some drink lager, some cider and many prefer wine
WKD and Malibu are favourites of mine
Some people have a problem and can't drink at all
while others drink until the last call
However you take it, alcohol is a drug
those that keep doing it, people think are mugs
But an alcoholic doesn't choose to live this way
after all, I'm only having my say

Smart Phone

A necessity now is a smart phone
it's a way of life now, don't condone
We used to use the call box that was red
going in there now, we wouldn't be seen dead
Phones going off now wherever we are
and you still see some on theirs in the car
For the over 40's, facebook is the latest fad
put your life on there, you must be sad
I drive all over the place using google maps
although on my phone I have many apps
Samsung or Iphone, for you which one?
Iphone for me, the deal is done
My phone does everything except talk to me
that will happen soon, you'll see
Pay bills, take pictures it does it all
we hardly use them to make calls
Our smart phone is our new best friend
if you have one, it's something you will never lend
We keep our phones close by us at all times
I have my screensaver to tell it's mine

Autism

So many more get diagnosed each year
nobody knows why, it isn't clear
Social interactions are very hard for them
and sometimes it becomes too much, and it's all mayhem
An autistic person likes to stick to routine
anything new, they are never very keen
Some are in residential as they are so bad
for their families, this is so sad
What causes autism? A faulty gene
screening soon will be very much routine
Someone with autism needs understanding and help
stop and think how their parents have felt
A lot more resources are very much needed
I expect most parents have all pleaded
The government needs to walk in their shoes
and then listen to the parents views
Cut backs is all we hear about now
give them more help if you'll allow

Loneliness

How do we measure what loneliness is
Is it no one to give you a cuddle and a kiss
Could it be sitting in at night on your own
or could it be no one on the end of the phone
It could be having no one to go out with for a drink
loneliness can leave you right on the brink
I miss my old life and the friends that I had
but back then, I was oh so mad
How many people are lonely like me
ask around and you'll see
People rush about not thinking of anyone else
think of others, not just yourself
The deadliest enemy is how a suicidal person sees loneliness
but someone like this should be treated with kindliness
Try to talk about how you feel
although opening up, can be quite an ordeal
When you're lonely, you don't feel understood or cared for
You are so sad and down that before long your tears will pour
You think nobody can empathise with you
but really, you haven't got a clue
Lets help anyone we think is sad and alone
after all, it's really not fun being on your own

50

I'm 50 years old and feel like shit
this is something I'm finding hard to admit
I'm old and lonely, living in a strange place
I look in the mirror and feel a disgrace
Today, someone said I have a sadness about me
when I hear this, I want to turn around and flee
Would I do things different if I had a chance
my life, I need to enhance
50 is the new 40 or so they say
although these days, most of my days are grey
Am I ready to make new friends and start again
starting again is such a drain
Can I be bothered getting to know someone
at the moment, most people, I just shun
I am alone but too lazy to change it
I'll change things slowly bit by bit
I get interviews for jobs, and I don't even go
I need to get better and go with the flow
I go out and don't speak and never make eye contact
acting like this, friends, I'll never attract
People I meet, think I am so sad
but am I sad, bad or perhaps even mad
This has been my worst birthday so far
to be honest, the whole year is on par
I cry each day, but always when I'm alone
loneliness is hard, would I have moved here if I had known
I'm going to get well, and be a new person by spring
and hopefully happiness it will bring

Christmas

Christmas now, is on the way
so much expense, all for just a day
The kids want more, each and every year
but I look about and everything is so dear
The shops are filled with tinsel and glitter
I walk about, but it's so cold and bitter
Children get excited and write letters to Santa Claus
they shout and scream and don't stop for a pause
It's commercialised now and that's a sad fact
but we buy what we can, while keeping it intact
The turkey is cooked and we sit and enjoy
cook it too long and you might destroy
We toast the queen with a glass of sherry
we keep on drinking and get rather merry
Bloated and full is how we go to bed
this feeling I hate and always dread
With my family I will spend the day
let's have a white one, we all pray

Theatre

Musicals is the thing for me
I take my seat and wait and see
The curtain opens, and out comes the cast
going to the theatre, I always have a blast
I sing along to the songs that I know
last time I went was ages ago
The costumes are colourful and very bright
every so often sequins catch the light
I've been so many times, I've lost count
and the more you go, there's no discount
The gold leaf paint always catches my eye
there's no paint here that would drip dry
The curtains are red and so very old
most are originals, or so I'm told
The stairs are narrow and so very grand
when you get to the top, you're too scared to stand
The orchestra is at the front, right by the stage
some in there are in their teens, while others are a golden age
The production has now come to an end
I'm sad it has finished and I can't pretend
I wonder if I'll ever come back
someone to accompany me, is what I lack

The Motorway

On the motorway cars rush past me
the queue is as far as the eye can see
different colours pass me by
so many colours, why oh why
I put my foot down and increase my speed
before very long, I'm in the lead
Cars are fast, cars are slow
some take their time, even so
The motorway is miles and miles long
I drive along listening to a song
The journey is long and can be a bore
my son is asleep with his head on the door
Back on the A303 and homeward bound
the music is off and there's not a sound
Police and ambulances whizz on past
I can't believe how they drive so fast
The man on the sat nav speaks loud and clear
not long now and I'll be back in Mere
I've been driving about all through the day
still find it hard to find my way

Boobs

Boobs come in different shapes and sizes
some think it helps to do exercises
Some are not happy with the little bit they've got
while others aren't happy and have rather a lot
Some nipples are large and some are tiny
it's a subject we all find funny
Mine are too big, and have been the bain of my life
comments have given me nothing but strife
How much is enough? We all ask
although most men, like to see them spilling out of a basque
Bras now come in different styles
to get sexy colourful ones, I travel miles
Our boobs, for many make us feel good
would you part with them? If I had to, of course I would
If you have big boobs, it's very hard to run and jump
whatever your size, we all need to check for lumps

Dying

Dying, this is something that doesn't scare me
at least from the world, we will be free
My kids are older and have their own lives
some are scared and will do anything to survive
Sometimes I feel that my work here is done
would I feel the same, if there had been more fun
Is there something better than this life for us after
I want to go somewhere, where there's always laughter
Some days I'm so tired and just want to go
why do I feel this way, I don't really know
Family I have lost, will all be there to greet me
at times, this excites me, but I'll wait and see
A humanist funeral is what I want when I die
I'm happy to talk about it and won't even cry
George Michael singing, and no one in black
I think about my life often and have the odd flashback
A celebration of some one's life, is what a funeral is
keep it as they would want, and remember this
Stresses and strains have wore me out
I'm broken and sad and can't be bothered to go out and about
But I'm happy now to wait until it's my time
after all, waiting to go, isn't really a crime

Lies

I'm hurt beyond belief with the way you are
You act so different all the time, you are quite bizarre
Why do I keep going back for more
when you treat me like something you stepped off the floor
I've decided now to cut all ties
I realise now all you did was lie
You totally ruined the person I was
I'm a good person, It's you who has the flaws
Go to the next one and lie away
I wish I could warn them, as you make a play
You use women, and you really disgust me
the good thing is I am now free
You dragged me down, and I lost all I had
when I think what you've done to me, I get very mad
I am just one in a huge list for you
Go on out there and pick someone new
You seduced me with the lies that came out of your mouth
I now know everything you said was an untruth

In Love

Being in love feels so good
I would feel like this forever if I could
Butterflies in your tummy
make us feel so yummy
Can't eat, can't sleep at any time
I've had my chance, I'm past my prime
They are constantly on your mind
and at times when they treat you so kind
You can't think, you can't eat
you can't wait till you meet
You feel giddy and young
and at times highly strung
In love, is it the best feeling ever?
to answer this, you don't have to be clever
I don't want much, just to be treated as I should
if it happens, wouldn't it be good

My Team

The football season is fast upon us
we all love the game and have much to discuss
Which player will go to which team
give us someone good, that is our dream
We want our team in the top flight
but in the championship, things are so tight
Automatic promotion is what we all dream
they let in goals, bad defence, but they are our team
New players coming in all the time
some are even in their prime
Football is not the sport it used to be
play crap, and they let you go on a free
A manager is under so much pressure now
if only I could manage, would they allow
Who will go up and who will go down
glory is there, open top bus, through the town

The Shop

The shop is busy, the shop is dead
we need more customers, some have said
The sun is shining and I want to be elsewhere
running about free, without a care
I watch the trains rushing past
I want to catch it, but would have to run too fast
The radio plays Wham and I'm in heaven
god I'm bored already, been here since seven
Customers moaning, customers happy
some are aggressive while others are snappy
I can't even entice people to come on in
I'll get them in, yes I'll win
I push the products without a care
anyone can do it, if they dare
Scratchcards and papers is all they buy
I try to read the headlines, I'm not gonna lie
I listen to their stories and they come back for more
yet sometimes I want to show them the bloody door
The alcoholics are in buying can after can
while I'm standing here thinking I wish I had a fan
I'm so bored today, my head is on tonight
I'll have some fun with all my might

Summer's End

The summer is over and Dawlish is a ghost town
the only place still busy is the Landsdowne
I came here months ago now, when I was ill
but I've slowly made friends and started to heal
some customers have been good for me and restored my trust
the way they are with me, I'd go out with them if I must
The locals talk of the storms years ago
some live in the past, even so
I walk the wall and look out to sea
some days, I want people to just leave me be
I need to meet people and get on out there
but most of the time, I couldn't care
A new life is what I have to make here
but my memories I hold so close and so dear
Dawlish is now the place I call home
some hate it here, but we mustn't moan

Men

I haven't had a good experience with a man
they hurt you and cheat if they can
they say there are some good ones out there
go and look for one, I couldn't care
Some sit in the pub, downing pints of beer
while others are caring and treat you so dear
Men confuse me most of the time
while some have men who go out and commit crimes
I want a man to look after me
I'm too tired to look, so it will never be
Some men are loud, fight and act wild
while others are quiet, calm and act mild
Some have stubble, which turns me on
some have beards which they wear so long
I like my man to have dark hair
while some women like their man to be fair
Good manners is definitely a must
while others like theirs with plenty of lust

Clothes

We wear the clothes that we like the best
we choose our outfit and get dressed
Trousers or a dress, what do I choose
some pick their outfit, then the shoes
Our clothes represent the person that we are
some go out dressed very bizarre
some men go out dressed in a dress
all dolled up to impress
Clothes are worn like a second skin
and some of the sights we see, make us grin
We buy online or go to the shops
some have friends with clothes to swap
mums and daughters go out in the same outfit
while others go out looking like a misfit
We spend a lot of money on our clothes
then try them all on, and do a pose
Sometimes it's nice to wear a skirt
if it's long, it sometimes drags in the dirt
There's all different colours of the rainbow
but what suits you, only you know

Immigration

Immigration laws in this country suck
ask our government, they don't give a fuck
How can you attempt to deport someone whose lived here
55 years
there's a lot more stories of this, and that's my fear
Someone that has been here since the age of five
he probably wishes now, he had never arrived
In this country, he attended school
our bloody government, you're nothing but fools
He married and raised a family in this country
at times, I feel he is being treated quite abruptly
He's worked all his life, and very successful at his job
ask him how he feels, and he'll never open his gob
In taxes, he's paid thousands of pounds
but from him, we are not hearing a sound
The government do not care, he has no home to go to
and how is he feeling, they don't have a clue

My Plan

The next two years I have a plan
I will work, work, work and save all I can
I will make memories with family and friends
and with some I'll have to make amends
I've tried so hard to get on and be happy
but the loneliness does nothing but make me snappy
I'm sick to death of being on my own
the kids don't need me, they've all outgrown
I want a man to love me and look after me
but that will never happen, its plain to see
This life is not for me now
but my plan, the kids would never allow
So I will work and save and quietly plan
I want to go back to where it all began
I've tried so hard to act normal and sane
but perhaps I really am mad or is it my brain
I wasn't made to live my life alone
it's so hard starting again, and I have no backbone
The pain will all go one day soon
and I will be looking down at you all from the moon

War

This is the state of armed conflict between societies
thinking of war causes amense anxieties
It is generally extreme aggression, destruction and mortality
but war just brings more and more fatality
The deadliest war was the second world war
Hitler wanted it all, to rule the world, more and more
In 2013, war resulted in 31,000 deaths
but the idiots that start war are nothing but pests
War usually results in a big decrease in social spending
when war is raging it's never ending
Asmmetric, biological and chemical are all types of warfare
all of this, to us, does nothing but scare
The Syrian war has been going on for 6 years
people killed, people hurt, and some just sit and shed tears
Kim Jong Un would declare war everyday if he could
someone needs to stop him soon, if they would
Donald Trump is also eager to fight
although most of his talk, is said to fright
2 months the Falklands war lasted
it was over so quick, it could be one of the fastest
We hear of families at war all the time
but families at war, it isn't a crime

Drugs

I smell cannabis wherever I go now
the police, all know, I think they allow
People walk about as high as kites
could this be the start of an awful plight
It normally starts with a bit of weed
until they end up with a bigger need
Before long, they are on heroin and crack
they sometimes lose it all and live in a shack
And all too soon, they are injecting each day
selling anything, so that they can pay
Legal highs is the latest fad
I never went down that road, I'm so very glad
It can start with a joint and before you know it
you have become a full blown addict
Stealing and lying to pay for the gear
hiding around corners, living in fear
This is not a life for anyone
people look, and then they shun
Educate the youngsters on the dangers of drugs
go into schools, talk, set up clubs
Cleanse our youths of this awful pastime
do this, and you'll see a drop in crime

Love

Love is a word that is often used
the word just leaves me very confused
People use the word and hurt each other
while others use it from one to another
How can your feelings change so quick?
Or is it another one of your tricks?
Love is used every single day
not from my lips, there's no way
I've never used this word on a man
I never will now, that's my plan
People say it with the drop of a hat
some say it too much, and that's a sad fact
In the beginning you chat and then flirt
you give your heart and then get hurt
If you've been let down and it's hard to trust
give it a try, if you must
rather than love, I use the word like
I'll suss you out at first, though I'm no psych
Look after your heart, so it can't break
watch your guard, or it's someone's to take

Smoking

So the government is now banning packets of ten
what about the revenue they get from each pack then
They want everyone to kick the fags
If it's not the government, it's the drs, nag nag nag
Being told what to do, is it wrong?
Perhaps I want one, which is what I long
We are not allowed to smoke at work now
If we want one, we have to go off site and get back somehow
A packet of cigarettes had got so dear
Smokers moaning, that's all we hear
More people will buy duty free
This will get out of hand, you'll see
There will also be many packets of fakes
The police will be busy, taking packets, and even a keepsake
I'm so glad I never started to smoke
But to be told you can't, what a joke

Ageing

Old age is starting to creep up on me
will I be all wrinkled, I'll wait and see
My hands have a few age spots
a few more years and they'll be lots and lots
I get hot flushes now at night
god I must look an awful sight
The menopause for me is almost in my past
I've been symptom free, god I hope it lasts
I don't rush about now, I do things much slower
and don't forget, we have to get that blood pressure lower
I have asthma now and issues with my heart
the Dr says don't stress, and all I'm thinking is don't start
I wish I could turn the clock back 10 years
would I still be alone, yes I fear
I'm days from turning 50 and this makes me sad
I'll go out, have a drink and act bad
We all get old and cannot change it
I wish I could, at least for a bit

Running Away

In our lives many of us run away
some don't and in their lives forever stay
What I run away from, you may not
Some stay put and end up getting very fraught
People run away for all sorts of reasons
but all you are doing is hiding from your demons
I ran away and had to start all over again
it was the hardest thing, but I had to break that chain
Running away is always as easy as it seems
you run away and you are full of dreams
First you need to sort out what you are running from
think about the future and not what your life has become
Life can be hard, but we all have things to face
we all want happiness and to be in a good place
So sometimes the answer is not to always run
stay put, and sort things out, until all is done

Happy

How do you know if you are happy or sad
today I feel happy and feel so glad
Have you ever been so low, you can't get out of bed
waking up each morning, with feelings of dread
I want to be happy and feel warm inside
this past year, oh yes I've tried
When we are happy, we show pleasure and contentment
sad, unhappy people only show resentment
Merry, cheerful and carefree are ways we can feel happy
it's better to be happy, than walking around feeling crappy
Happiness can predict longevity and wealth
a happy person is usually in good health
Everyone has the power to make small changes in their behaviour
if not, you could end up a failure
Our surroundings and relationships help set us on course for a happier life
we all want happiness and not the strife
Happiness normally comes from within
but you've got to love yourself to begin
Optimism is how each day should be approached
get this right, and you're forever happy, well almost

Geralds 2017

This summer, Geralds is the place where I did work
Bernard, Karen and Aimee run it like clockwork
Sue has worked here for many many years
and inside out she knows her peers
Rory is the joker among the pack
he's even worse, when he works with Jack
Ed is composed and a quiet young man
he really is the quietest of the clan
BJ is here, but his heart is with the army
good for him, although, some would think barmy
Denise lives close by and loves her job
even at times when her knees throb
Terry and Amy are loves young dream
watching them together, they make a good team
University is calling Jess and Jade
let's hope they both get their grades
Some customers are good and some are bad
Jo works many hours and is there most days
ask her and she wouldn't have it any other way
Katherine is my favourite among the staff
although, with all of them, I've had a laugh
Sophie's going travelling all on her own
fly the nest, but always give your mum a phone
Helen lives above the shop and works like a dog
if you're up and about early, you'll see her out for a jog
I pushed those biscuits, making a few customers mad
they all got sold, of which I'm glad
The summer was great and we all had a blast
it's a shame that the season cannot last

Lonely

I'm so lonely and so sad
why am I like this, am I bad
Some days I awake and all looks black
there must be something that I lack
Some days I want to end it and go to sleep
these are my feelings, for me to keep
I hide it well, and put on a fake smile
I wish I could say how I feel, once in a while
People are busy and don't want to listen to me
will I ever be as I was, I'll wait and see
I'm damaged now and have to live this way
even though most of my days are grey
If I could go to sleep and never wake
surely you can see, this is my choice to make

Birds

The seagull sits on the chimney looking in at me
I look out slowly, where there was one is now three
I have the biggest phobia of birds
if they come near me I can be heard
Their feathers I don't even like to touch
sometimes my screaming becomes too much
Pigeons swoop when I walk past
I start to panic and my heart beats fast
even the black swans, I don't go near
birds really is my worst fear
Feathers fill the duvet on my bed
when one comes out, to pick it up, I dread
I'm an animal lover, so would never hurt one
but get near one, I'd rather run
Owls scare me, the way their head turns around
looking for mice, swooping to the ground
Well my phobia is birds, and it will never change
some laugh at me, and some think I'm strange

Bed

My bed is my favourite place
it is my very own personal space
my bed has big fluffy heart cushions
I want to find more, that's my mission
At night I stretch out like a queen
watching me, would be quite a scene
I love my bed and my pretty quilt
I'm careful when I drink in bed, so nothing is spilt
My bed is girly and very pink
no man to tell me what to do, wink wink
I use my bed to sit and write
When I sit there at night, I put on the light
I love my bed with all my heart
get rid of it, we will never part
It's comfortable and a nice size
it's mine, and was one of my best ever buys

NHS

The NHS is at breaking point
operations getting cancelled, it's just disappoint
You go to A + E and end up in the corridor on a trolley
you get moved and pushed about, as if you were on a jolly
The NHS is running out of cash fast
soon we will be paying, whatever is asked
They say now, no treatment if you smoke
but what happens if you have a stroke?
Everything seems to be means tested now
it's our NHS, should this, we allow
We will be paying to see a dr before long
this is also very wrong
You're in hospital, and you're out in a day
let the public have their say
They waste money, without a care
All we can do for the NHS is say a little prayer

ADHD

What makes you behave in this way
loud, hyped up for most of the day
We give you pills to calm you down
but 100% of the time you act like a clown
Most people just think you are a naughty kid
let them say that to me, god forbid
I was called into school countless times
and then there was the petty crimes
ADHD is a condition and it's real
as a parent, it was hard, I can imagine how you feel
You're older now, with a family of your own
although as a kid, you were never alone
Concerta XL was the drug you took
I know all about it, I could write a book
You're older now and off your meds
I'm embarrassing you now, enough has been said

What am I

I am a daughter to my mum and dad
I once was a wife, but that now makes me sad
To my beautiful children, I am a mother
looking back now, I wish I had of had another
I am a sister to Paul and I am a bit older
as young adults, all his problems, I did shoulder
I have many cousins and we all live miles apart
I think of them often and it warms my heart
I have aunties and uncles and to them I am a niece
not so many now, as some have sadly deceased
My greatest joy is being a nanny with another on the way
I'm so excited and on countdown to that special day
We all have a purpose on this earth
which goes a long way to our self worth

Past

My room is packed with pictures from my past
I have memories, and hope they last
We all have a past, good or bad
I think about some things and get very sad
My children are my greatest joy
Let's hope my memory doesn't destroy
I look at pictures and start to cry
Before very long, I have to dry my eyes
My pictures tell a beautiful story
In albums and in boxes in all their glory
Some of the things we did was wrong
But forget that now, and act strong
Some of the things we did was good
These I want to remember, as I should
Some memories are painful, and stay in our mind
Some days I want to talk about them, it helps to unwind
But our past is ours and ours alone
Whatever it is, we mustn't condone

Goodbye

I've had enough and want to say goodbye to this earth
I've been here nearly 50 years since my birth
Goodbye to all of my family and my friends
anyone I've fallen out with, I make amends
Goodbye to all the lovely memories I have made
I'll be going soon and I'm not afraid
Goodbye to everything that I have ever done
all the bad times and the fun
Goodbye to any man that has ever hurt me
no more pain, just you see
Goodbye to all the jobs I have done in my life
a job I once had was being a wife
Goodbye to husbands, it wasn't all bad
I'm single now, which I'm sometimes glad
Goodbye to my possessions and all that I have worked hard for
all these goodbyes are making my eyes sore
Goodbye to all the values that I hold so dear
this for me has been my most painful year
Goodbye to my life, I'm happy to go
think of me and don't get low
Hello to my new life in the clouds
it's been good, but I'm going and I'm allowed

Nurses

I sit in my hospital bed and watch the nurses hard at work
rushing about without a care, anyone else would go berserk
They do their job without a single moan
not even from the students, do you hear a groan
dressings, bloods all to do, and sometimes there's even a swab
this is all in a day of a nurses job
a nurse in our country is very underpaid
and each of them worked hard to get their grade
They use agency as not enough are trained
carrying on like this, nothing can be gained
We need more nurses, and that's a sad fact
the government needs to stop getting side tracked
The NHS needs a lot more money
this is so sad and really not funny
Before very long, we will all have to pay
many many people are scared of that day
Work out a plan, so more can be trained
otherwise the NHS will continue to be drained

Rejection

In life, how much rejection can one person take
thinking of my life, my heart aches
My kids reject me as have men
ask them and they'd probably say when
Why does this happen, am I so bad
I'm scared and lonely and at times very sad
I expect the worst now all the time
some of my life has been like a pantomime
I find it very hard to trust anyone now
I need to let somebody in, somehow
I almost want people to treat me like dirt
but with men, I can't trust, I've been so very hurt
how many times can one person be rejected
a few for me, but I have been affected
Who rejected you, a husband, a wife, a partner or a lover
some even get rejected by their mother
When you get rejected, be strong and walk away
don't give them the satisfaction of having their day

Donald Trump

What do we feel about Donald Trump
for me, I would like to see him get thumped
Some say he is an American success story
marching about with his yellow hair in all his glory
He started his business way back in New York City
and all too soon he had his own committee
He is the 45th president of the United States
he certainly will never be one of the greats
Trump is mad and just wants war
Kim Jong Un and him should both be shown the door
Put them both on an island so they can fight til the end
on twitter this would certainly trend
They are both very evil men
they're on the news, in the papers, I'm thinking not again
Trump has paid to get where he is
talking about him, I'll give it a miss

Failure

Is failure a lack of success
this is something we shouldn't guess
Could it be being a flop
think of it, and you'll end up in a strop
A failure is someone who doesn't succeed
they try so hard, they do indeed
or could you just be, a born loser
As long as you don't end up down the boozer
Failing to perform a duty or expected action
although for some, this is an attraction
Did you fail to get the job of your dreams
sometimes it's not all as it seems
Did you fail at school to get your grades
for some, they will still end up with a trade
Did you go bankrupt and lose the business you had
times like that, are just so sad
Was the accident caused by a failure to use correct procedures
people will point and talk, but they won't know either
Could you or me be suffering from heart failure
look after your heart, it's very major
Crop failure can be caused by drought
you look about and nothing starts to sprout
Failure is such a nasty word
don't use it, yes that's right, you heard
We are all unique in whatever we do
but a failure, I really think not, do you

Homelessness

Everywhere I go, there are people living rough
for anyone, this must be so very tough
Nobody in this country should be living this way
perhaps the powers that be should try it for a day
These people sleep in shop doorways, trying to keep warm
but there's no escape for them, even when we have a storm
What is wrong with our nation, allowing people to live like this
Try and talk to the government and you will be dismissed
These people all have a story, and some have lost more than most
it's nothing to be proud of, and none of them will ever boast
People sleep on the beach, under the pier
there's more coming all the time, each and every year
Everyone in this country deserves to have a roof over their head
not being in some doorway, with feelings of dread
If everyone in this country donated a pound, we could house these people
or is this idea, nothing but feeble
New houses could be built which in turn would create jobs
here I go again, me and my bloody gob

Pain

What is pain and how does it hurt you
Is it someone hitting you with a shoe
Could it be someone breaking your heart
Could it be realising you are not as smart
Pain could be losing a loved one
Someone shooting you with a gun
What is pain and how do you measure it
When someone can't fit into their favourite outfit
The next person to be diagnosed with cancer
Someone else could phone a partner and get no answer
Whatever it is, it is your pain and yours alone
However it hurts you, we mustn't condone
Pain affects us in different ways
What hurt me yesterday, may not today
My pain is mine to deal with how I see fit
I will think about this as a stay here and sit

Scratch Cards

What is the fascination with a scratch card
some play so much that they get barred
Some buy £10 ones, while others have £5 ones
playing these cards is meant to be someone's fun
Most people buy the ones that are 2 and 3 pound
they leave the shop clutching them, not making a sound
They are all hoping that they will win
but the cards the winner, I look away and grin
Some have an addiction and spend pounds on this
they do this as they pray for that win, surely something's a miss
Some can't even leave the shop, before they are scratching them off
I watch them waste their money and stand with a nervous cough
The colours lure the public to buy
some get so mad, they almost cry
I think they are all a waste of money
but watching them is rather funny
Most that win nearly always buy more
some lose and end up nearly kicking the door

Abortion

So women in Scotland can now take the abortion pill
the government will have to rewrite the bill
This will mean only one visit to the doctors for these people
while all the time we are talking fetal
The pill can be taken at the same time with a gap of a few days
at least now, women can have their way
The abortion act came in 50 years ago
and this act, has had many people come to blows
This gives women the right to terminations that are safe
without them going to a back street place
The pill is used to induce a miscarriage
and now they don't have to feel disparage
Pills can be used up to 24 weeks
and many women now have the freedom of speech
What I or you believe doesn't come into it
It's up to them what they do, and we have to permit
This must be the worst decision for anyone to make
and for some, it's just heartache
The new act is about freedom of choice
and letting these women have a voice

Marriage

My marriage ended after 18 years
at the time, I went out and had a few beers
The marriage died as we grew apart
so for me now, I have to make a fresh start
Today we are civil and remain friends
but ending a marriage, you need to cleanse
Do I feel sad that it has ended
it's over I think, how very splendid
I've had two marriages and I feel shame
at times, I feel I am the one to blame
Would I ever love to meet the man of my dreams
I wish, but nothing is as ever as it seems
For many years I was a wife
actually it's more than half my life
For some people, they stay together for ever
try to separate them, it will never sever
I think I am doomed to stay alone
when I was younger I wish I had of known
I've had two husbands and neither did I love
but change it, only the lord above
I'm only being honest about how I feel
at the time, marriage, it did appeal
But now I realise it only brings heartache
they reel you in and your heart will break

Flowers

How many times do you get flowers in your life
you normally get plenty, when you're a wife
On Mother's day, your children might buy you some
if you're lucky, you may get some from a chum
On valentine's day, you get them from your lover
we all want this to last forever
On your birthday, friends could buy you a bunch
while others prefer to take you out for lunch
Flowers or a plant, what do you choose
you get flowers in your room, when you're on a cruise
Flowers make us feel good, like someone's cares
some even use flowers to decorate their hair
At our funeral, we get flowers whoever we are, whatever we do
receiving flowers lifts our mood, and we certainly don't ever feel the blues
However we receive flowers, they make us feel good
perhaps we all need to buy more, yes I think we should

Euthansia

This is a subject we all have an opinion about
and of this, I'm definitely in no doubt
In different countries, there are different euthanasia laws
but opting for this has to be the last straw
This is when a deliberate intervention is undertaken to end life
but for the one's left behind, this cuts like a knife
The Dutch law does not use this term
and for some, they can't listen and just squirm
They used assisted suicide & termination of life on request
but you have to do what's right for you, only you know best
It can be voluntary, non voluntary or involuntary
although it goes on, it's still rather exploratory
Voluntary is legal in some cases
but it all depends on the exact places
Non voluntary is illegal everywhere
this is something, that is really very rare
Involuntary is considered murder and very much illegal
this is something in my life, that will never be legal
I think we all have the right to decide when to die
go off to the heavens and fly so high
Nobody wants to be here, as a burden to anyone
after all, their poor life, would be no such fun

Sleep

How much is enough sleep
Some people can't and have to count sheep
Do you sleep right through the night
I amost do, but not quite
How many hours do we need
8 hours the experts have agreed
Some people sleep and snore so loud
Whiles others talk as if they're in a crowd
Most of the night, some people will dream
Our dreams are never as they seem
During the day, we try to remember
It's all jumbled up, the great pretender
Some people cat nap all night long
While others are up all night playing songs
However you sleep, it's something we all need to do
So lie back, count sheep, it's true

Downs Syndrome

Trisomy1 is also known as downs syndrome
a lot of these people live together in a home
It is a genetic disorder we cannot stop
but these children, I certainly wouldn't swap
It is normally associated with physical growth delays
can we stop this happening, there is no way
So 50 is the average IQ for someone with downs
years ago these people would have been disowned
They usually have a mental age of an 8/9 year old
they are so loving, and each has a heart of gold
They all tend to have delayed physical growth
physical and learning disabilities, most have both
Sometimes this happens when the mother is older
for some, this is too much to shoulder
Some pregnancies are terminated when the parents find out
these people are worth their weight in gold, of this I'm in no doubt
They are the most loving people I have ever met
and to society they are definitely an asset
They tend to have poor immune function among other things
spend a day with a person with downs and they will pull at your heart strings

Memories

The memories we have, are locked in our mind
sometimes, we see things and it starts to unwind
Some of us have good memories and some are so bad
some do nothing, except make us sad
A memory can be dormant for many many years
you start to remember, and it's not always what it appears
Some people live in the past and can't move on
but for them, it's what they do long
Whatever your memory, it is unique to you
Some memories stick to you like super glue
I have memories that I wish would just go
why do they stick in my mind? I don't really know
We have memories of our childhood
all of these memories are so very good
A memory is something that is stored in our brain
but some memories are nothing but a pain
We all make memories each and every day
cherish them all, we can but pray

Spring

Spring is on the way and it makes us feel good
I'd have the summer all year round if I could
Animals are coming out of hibernation and the plants are growing
we still get days of wind and rain and all hat blowing
There's lambs running about in the fields now
and out in all weather's is the poor cow
I like the summer and have always done
laying out somewhere, enjoying the sun
They say the sun is good for our mind
laying there sunbathing, my eyes feel so blind
We are all so moody with all the wind and the rain
but we have to put up, to get to summer, yes it's a pain
The grass is growing, the trees are now so green
things are getting ready for the summer season, all is now clean
Spring is the season that makes us feel good
I'd have summer all year, if I could
We all know, it's not long and summer will be here
children out playing, it's the best time of year
I hate the cold and all it brings
but the world was made this way, it's one of those things
Spring is truly definitely on the way
I can't wait and I'm counting the days

Feelings

Are you happy or are you sad?
Are you good or are you bad?
How do you feel on this day?
Doom or gloom or happy and gay
Our feelings are unique to each and every one
but however I or you feel it can't be outdone
I feel frustrated at certain times
sad that I'm old and past my prime
Passion, sentiment, desire, infatuation and lust
while others feel disgust and often mistrust
Excitement and pleasure we like, says our brain
while others experience nothing but pain
How do we measure how we feel
some refuse, and end up talking spiel
It's good to experience different thoughts
when you feel scared your stomach is in knots
Being in love can give you butterflies
so very happy at times, you feel so high
When sad you cry and hurt so very much
the tears come when someone gives you a slight touch
However you feel, it is up to you
and this I'm afraid is very true

Hair

How do you wear your hair? Long or short
you tie it back when you play sport
Is your hair dark or is it light
although if you dye it, you have to get it just right
Hair can be curly or straight
mine is straight, which I hate
Which shampoo and conditioner do you choose
so much choice, it really does confuse
Wear it up or down, what do you do
at certain times, I really haven't a clue
You can perm your hair or even curl it
and think of those poor kids at school with the nits
For some their hair is their crowning glory
about their hair, most people have a story
Some wear turbans on their head
but for them, seeing their head, some do dread
You can buy pretty things to put in your hair
not for me though, I couldn't care
You do with your hair whatever you want
and get on out there and flaunt

Seasons Change

It's so cold and the sky is grey
the seasons have to change, that is the way
It feels so deep, and there's a chill in the air
but I'm working inside, so I don't really care
Christmas is coming and people are hoping for snow
why do people love it, that's something I don't really know
Christmas for me, will be different this year
although the good think is, I'm no longer in Mere
My son is working, so I will be here alone
but some people have nothing, so I shouldn't moan
This time last year, I was so very happy
but I'm old, tired and most of the time snappy
Life is cruel and life is hard
but now I'm just so bloody scarred
I moved away to start afresh
but my life is one long emotional mess
Will I ever be the person I used to be
time is a great healer, I'll wait and see

My Son

My son is not a baby anymore
my love for him still soars
His voice is so deep and he towers over me
precious moments chatting, when you are free
He is a man now, with a woman of his own
he is happy, I am lonely, but I don't condone
It's hard for me watching and letting go
but my love for him just grows and grows
Long ago when he was a boy, he liked to play
on the playstation, all hours of the day
But he's all grown up now and goes out to work
he's always been a worker and never shirked
If I could, would I turn back time
at least then, I may have been in my prime
It is such precious time, when they are small
especially that day, when he learnt to crawl
My son I really am very proud of you
I'll end this now, as I'm feeling quite blue

Hate

What does it mean to hate
Like or love makes you feel great
But dislike and hate are not a nice way to feel
Is hate a feeling, is it real
What does it mean, to say I hate you?
Love and hate are so close, but so far it's true
You love one minute and hate the next
We all treat this word the same, whatever our sex
Hate is a very strong word to be used
With youngsters it's often abused
From now on, I will use dislike instead
I will try and drum it into my head
I don't like, I prefer to say
And from now on hate, I will move away
We hurt others by using this word
But from my mouth it will be unheard

Children

I have 3 children and they are all grown up now
Not it's time for me, that's a vow
One girl and two boys for me
Not the 2.4 like some, I had three
The house was always noisy with their play
Screaming, laughter, happy and gay
The washing machine was always on
It never stopped, but it always got done
They were always stripping the cupboards of food
You'd think I had a bigger brood
Monopoly was our favourite game
Except I always bought the same
Looking back their childhood was sound
Although at times they gave me the run around
The house is quiet now, as two have left
I sit here with the last one, totally bereft

Laughing

How many times can you laugh in a day
I'd laugh all day if I had my way
Is it comedy you laugh at
or do you laugh at anything from this to that
Do you laugh with others at yourself
what makes me laugh is the film Elf
Are you happy and just like to laugh
at work, it's good to share a joke with the staff
The experts say laughing is good for the heart
but we laugh at comedians, to when someone farts
Jack Dee and Peter Kay are favourites of mine
sit back and watch with a big glass of wine
As humans there's lots of things we all find funny
most funny things, don't cost any money
laughing is a tonic for all sorts of things
the drs should prescribe this, and see the happiness it brings
Try and have a laugh at least once a week
there's nothing better than hearing laugher and people shriek

Terror

The country is now on high terror alert
how low can you go and at a concert
someone has to be responsible for this mess
we are all shocked with no words to express
The government have made cuts in the police force
more crime about, less police, of course
Cut backs on mental health care
we cannot go on like this it isn't fair
Immigrants need to be thoroughly checked
of this we all need to accept
He came into our country and ruined people's lives
stamp out this sort of act, to which we strive
He was known to the authorities, but what did they do
it seems people in high places don't have a clue
This sort of thing is happening more and more
this is our country, protect it now or terrorism will soar

Lonely

I'm so lonely very much of the time
although I know I'm old and past my prime
All I do is work and sleep, work and sleep
and the odd night, I sit in and weep
Will my life always be this way
I hope not, but I will still pray
Should I have moved here, I'm not so sure
but my life now is one big bore
The nights are drawing in and I dread this time of year
the only good thing is Christmas is getting near
Christmas for me will never be the same
George Michael's death and no one to blame
Last Christmas is a song I will never be able to listen to
I think of last year, and my mood turns blue
The leaves have fallen and blown everywhere
children run through them without any care
Life is hard and I guess always will be for me
but I can go where I want, I am oh so free
I sit in my bed night after night and think how it's all changed
I have my family near me, thank god we are not estranged
Making friends is something that I have to do
where to meet these people, I haven't a clue

George Michael

It is one year without our dear George on this earth
people are still trying to work out his net worth
I miss him more now, than I did before
and my poor eyes are still so sore
Last Christmas is a song that I cannot even play
I hear it in shops and have to walk away
Today I'm sat in and playing his songs so loud
if George is watching, he will be so proud
His lovelies love him more than ever
the love we feel will never sever
I listen to his music and each time I still cry
I can't help this, although, I'm not gonna lie
I have his picture above my bed
and even now, I cannot believe that he is dead
Wouldn't it be great for just one more day
but sadly I know, we won't get our way
My house is packed with memorabilia from years before
and even now, I'm still collecting more
Out of them all, he was the best
his life was always full of zest
I have my memories which are all good
we wanted longer if we could
Gorgeous, sexy and oh so gay
change him, no keep him that way
Raise your glass tonight and think of him
a world without George, oh how grim

Storm

Britain is braced to be battered by the storm
stay indoors, we must all conform
Several shops have their sand bags out
in another 6 months, we'll be talking of drought
Gale force winds and high tide is due
will they get it right, I don't have a clue
Storm Brian is the name they are using
the name Brian I think is so amusing
With gusts of winds over 70 MPH
some places will lose all their power
Warnings of flooding and potential power cuts
I go out in the town, and all is shut
Several flood warnings across England and Wales
snippets are coming out, with not much details
Torrential rain and high winds are expected here
soon it will be gone, and we'll be in the clear
Waves are expected to go over sea defences
and all again, we think of the expenses
We are being warned to stay away from the coast
but this is our home, although we shouldn't boast
Yellow strong wind warnings are still in place
storm Brian has come at a deadly pace
Environment agency has issued several flood alerts
all we hope, is that all are unhurt

My Prince

How does it feel to lose a baby
over the years, I thought was there a chance, maybe
Hydrocephalus and spina bifida is what I lost my son to at
26 weeks
even now, I regret and wish I had of had a peak
In a few weeks it will be 30 years to the day
It makes me sad, we never had a chance to play
I think so much of the time, what if
I quietly sit and cry and cry and sniff
He would of been a man now, with a family of his own
but the sad fact is, my son doesn't even have a tombstone
He's up there watching what I do
we will be reunited soon, that much is true
He has one sister and two brothers
but I'm the one who misses him, his mother
But the guilt I feel as he has no name
he is my prince, but at the time it was shame
He is my son and my first born child
but back then, you gave birth and weren't even reconciled
The medics said he would of been still born
but would he? To this day I still mourn
I was put in to labour, in a room with just a bible
and the tears came, like a mass tidal
But he kicked and kicked all night long
he kicked and I cried, and the guilt, was I so wrong
I will never forget that night as long as I live
my son, my baby, we will meet again, if only you can
forgive

Summer

The summer season is approaching fast
no rain and long hot days, we hope it lasts
The sun is out and we all feel good
laying in the sun feels as good as it should
I've been out in the sun and topped up my tan
I'll do it each day if I can
I lay on the beach and the sun makes my body so hot
I love the sun and don't ask for a lot
children are laughing, and are happy out to play
To live like this, I wish each day
In this country the seasons are so wet
more rain than anything else, you bet
I'm getting old and now feel the cold
skiing, not for me, I'd never be so bold
I love the sun and how it makes me feel
it's nice to be out in the sun, having a meal

Alcoholism

The alcoholics are in the shop all day long
what a way to live, surely this is wrong
They wait for the shop to open to get their drink
some are so bad, they are on the brink
They talk to you and their speech is slurred
they can't even focus as it all looks blurred
I feel sad that people live this way
They need help, but cannot pay
all day long they sit on the green
this is their life, or so it seems
They drink to pass the time of day
and probably wouldn't have it any other way
By the end of the day, they usually run out of money
this for them, is by no means funny
Some sleep rough and are out in all weather
let's save these people and act together

Sooty

It's been 4 long emotional years without you by my side
I feel washed out with the amount that I've cried
I miss you more now, than I did back then
but one day, we will be together again
I miss you sitting on my lap, and going to sleep
and of course, how could we forget the gorgeous Sweep
I feel you are around me, each and every day
but without you here, my world is grey
I loved you with all of my heart
and I really thought we would never part
I wear your fur around my neck
and each day I touch it and just check
I'm excited for the time to be with you
and until then, my mood will be blue
Before husbands and kids it was only ever us
when I have a bad day, I have no one now to sit and discuss
My life changed, that day you left me
one more day with you, is what I plea
Sooty my darling beautiful girl that you were
sitting on me dribbling and of course your lovely purr
I'm getting older, and soon we will be reunited
and of course by this, I'm so excited

Trust

What does it mean to trust someone
always protect your heart from the one
Putting your faith in someone's belief
they will take your feelings, just like a thief
Relationships are built on mutual trust and respect
it's a two way thing, or it will affect
Could you be suspicious and not trust your man
try not to be paranoid if you can
Have you trusted in the past
we all want our relationships to really last
You could have been let down and can't trust again
it's all about trying to break that chain
Trust is always a two way thing
if you can trust, the happiness it will bring
If you don't have trust, you will have nothing
this can be upsetting and very crushing
If you cannot trust, I think you should remain single
stay single, but go out and mingle
I do not trust as I have been hurt
they start off with a kiss and a flirt
I will now live out my days alone
I'm ok with this I shouldn't moan

Child's View

Watching a Christmas film makes us feel so good
we sit and watch and remember our own childhood
We forget we are adults and dream of being a child again
I'm back there visiting santa again on the train
As a child, Christmas is oh so magical
but for some, it's just a day, and they act so casual
You visit santa in his grotto
and some places are filled with artificial snow
You leave carrots for the reindeer and santa a mince pie
You go to bed, hoping to see the sleigh in the sky
You hope and pray, you will get what you asked for
does the meaning of Christmas exist anymore
You write your letter, and then sit and wait
on Christmas eve, you definitely don't go to bed late
You get up early and see that's he's been
opening up presents, it's now the time to begin
This has been the best one ever
I won't forget this day, no never

Sad

Today I feel so very low
what can I do, where can I go
I want to be happy and get on with my life
my life just feels so much of strife
I want to switch off the light and forget it all
I crawl into bed and roll into a ball
I feel peaceful and safe in my bed
so much negativity in my head
No one understands how I feel
I just need time so I can heal
I'm old and now on my own
it's been so long I shouldn't moan
I've been hurt and don't trust anymore
thinking of it all, my heart is sore
Life is hard and not for me now
will I ever be happy, I hope, somehow
I'll go to work and act as like I should
I'll put on a smile and act so good
I'm tired and fed up and want to go
I'm mad, I'm mental, I don't really know
I'm lonely and so very sad
what did I ever do to feel so bad

Self Harm

Is having a tattoo known as self harm
is cutting your arms, to keep yourself calm
Harm can be done in many ways
the medics will learn more about it one of these days
You can harm yourself popping one too many pills
some can eat and eat until they've had their fill
Some go the other way and eat nothing at all
while others use drugs and alcohol
Self harm is at an all time high
most don't understand and ask that question, why
A self harmer will intentionally injure their body
some could even call it a hobby
They do this to cope with emotional distress
even when at times, they go to excess
A cry for help is what this is
if you know a self harmer, don't dismiss
You can get some help a number of ways
but be prepared to sit and have your say

Toothache

How does a toothache make you feel
I'm in so much pain, I can't even eat a meal
I've been up and down all night long
the pain is severe, but I have to be strong
The pain travels right up to your ear
at times I feel like I can't even hear
I'm brushing my teeth whenever I can
I need to find a dentist soon, that's my plan
Have I lost a filling or chipped a tooth
opening my mouth for all to see, how uncouth
Is it a rotten tooth, or an abscess
the pain is now really making me stress
The dentists here are not taking on anyone new
god knows why I haven't a clue
I've never had toothache like this before
the whole side of my face is really so sore
I'll find a dentist and get it sorted out
and that is something that I'm in no doubt

John Lennon

In 1940 John Lennon was born
even now, people still mourn
He was born and bred in Liverpool
kids of today, think that's so cool
He was a member of the Beatles group
this for him was a massive coup
He had two sons Julian and Sean
they are without a dad, now he has gone
He married Yoko Ono in 1969
and yes it made the headlines
For peace he held a two week bed in
When watching on TV, you had to grin
Mark Chapman shot him in 1980
looking back, you could see Chapman was shady
Lennon lives on through his music and sons
it wouldn't have happened if people couldn't buy guns

Vaping

An e cigarette is a handheld electric device
to use one though, you may need some advice
It is used to create the feeling of smoking
at least with his you won't end up choking
Vaping is what an e cigarette is used for
so many different kinds, and coming, there's more and more
Using an e cigarette, we are not certain of health issues
but people keep on vaping without having a clue
Vaping can help some smokers to quit
and in doing this, they should feel so fit
Vaping shops are popping up everywhere
tobacconists, how do they feel, do they care
I'm not really bothered one way or another
but I do worry about the kids, after all, I am a mother

Snow

People go mad with the talk of snow
why do people like it, I don't really know
It's damp and cold and really not for me
but for some, they love it, and go away to ski
Kids make snow balls and lots of snow men
dads go out building, and the kids all shout, "again"
Mums look for old trays, you can slide down the hills
Children flying down the hill, but all you can hear are the squeals
Everyone gets excited when the snow starts to settle
me, as soon as it's outside my door, I'm boiling the kettle
We don't get snow anymore, like we did back in the day
thank god I say, or I'd have to invest in a sleigh
The snow looks pretty covering all that it can
imagine being on holiday, and in a caravan
Sometimes snow accumulates into a snowpack and may drift
In some places, it's so deep, you have to use a ski lift
The snows not for me, I like the sun
with both of these weathers, we all have fun

Paige

My beautiful daughter is soon to be a mum
this I think is so awesome
In the beginning, your baby will sleep and it will cry
and you will question yourself and think why
You will hold it in your arms as your most precious gift
and when you are tired and so worn out, it will give you a lift
Who will it look like, Will or you?
Whoever it looks like, it will make us all coo
Paige you will be the best mum ever
I'm so very proud of you and will be forever
Will it be a little girl or a little boy
whatever it is, will bring you such joy
You will nurture this baby and hold it tight
and cherish it with all of your might
I'm sad I was so ill when you found out
but I'm here for you now, I'm in no doubt
I'm getting stronger each day and ready to be a nanny again
this new baby will help to keep me sane
Paige I love you, I'm proud of you and I'm sorry for any pain I've caused
but we are humans, and many of us are flawed

Farewell

The last year you have been a constant in my life
to take you out of it, cuts like a knife
I know I have to move on and let you go
even though my feelings for you just grow and grow
I'm ok now and really over you
but how I still feel if only you knew
I'm prepared to let you go, which may hurt me
but you know where I am, I'll always wait and see
Get on with your life, and do what you must
my life without you, is such an unjust
I know you will be cross, but I'm saying goodbye
you know how I feel, I'm not gonna lie
I would wait for you forever in a day
My world without you in it, is so very grey
I would of looked after you, and treated you well
but I can't keep on, I mustn't dwell
It's so sad that we never did date
we got on so well, but it's never too late
Thank you for everything over the last year
not getting up and texting you, just gives me fear
You to me are everything that I want in a man
a carbon copy of you, that's my plan
I can't have you, so I'll stay on my own
here she goes again, you will probably moan
I live with my feelings buried very very deep
and the memories are mine to always keep

Death

It breaks our heart when our love one dies
they leave us, and fly high into the skies
Will they go to heaven, or go to hell
at least we don't know where we're going, which is just as well
A burial or a cremation, what will you choose
when someone dies, we get the blues
A funeral should be a celebration, not sat there in black
you sit and think about the past, and often have a flashback
To live forever, if there was a way
Eternal life, find a cure if you may
There's got to be a better life than this
back with all your family, oh the bliss
Is there such a thing as a ghost?
I nearly saw one once, almost
Most of us are scared of death
I'm not, although I won't hold my breath
dying is the start of something new
you were too good for this planet, I always knew

Rolf Harris

As children we loved to watch Rolf Harris paint
but his world came crashing down, when along came the complaints
He's performed in front of the queen several times
but now he's more remembered for his crimes
Paedophile is what some now call him
acting as he did, was he really that dim?
He's out of prison now, but life will never be the same
and he only has himself to blame
A digeroodo he was once famous for
we all loved it and wanted more
but now he is tainted for the rest of his life
and stood by him, has his silly wife
I saw him at the golden jubilee
he was proud to be there, and stood right in front of me
A union jack shirt he wore that day
but now, we think of all the girls that were his prey
They now say, he was innocent or an idiot, neither I think
Rolf Harris on the stage again, never ever will he return from the brink

Old Self

Today I feel like my old self and good
I knew I'd get there, of course I would
I was in a very dark place
I wanted no one near me just my space
I spent my days in my bed
my kids come into my room with dread
I'm in a good space now, and want this to stay
to feel like this, I want each day
Nobody understands, when you are so low
you prey and hope for the feelings to go
But it's like a big dark cloud over you
and why this happens, we have no clue
I've never felt this way before
I don't want to go back there anymore
Is it really the answer to pop a pill
although they make us feel so brill
Talking therapy is the way to go
that is something that I'm in the know

Autumn

Autumn is fast approaching us
we have Christmas to look forward to, that's a plus
The nights are dark with a chill in the air
people rushing about everywhere
The leaves are falling from the trees
children run about kicking them in the breeze
Will we get snow? Or more rain this year
if we get it, will it be mild or very severe
Acorns falling remind me of my childhood
I'd savour the memories if I could
In America they call it the fall
autumn for me brings the football
Orange is the colour that the berries turn
then it's Halloween, and we watch the guy burn

My Life

I've moved to Devon and finding things hard
I'm lonely and scared and a little bit scarred
I need to make friends to have a better life
just lately my life has been nothing but strife
I go to the pub and have a laugh and a drink
there's got to be something better, I often think
I hate my life and living here
it's got to the stage where I don't even care
Addicts and alcoholics hang outside the shop
people walk past scared, but do you see a cop
My life will never be what it once was
I'm old, damaged and now have many flaws
Some days I get up and don't want to be here
but being here is better than being back in Mere
Some days I'm so sad I can't even get out of bed
I've cried and cried and feel all my tears have been shed
Will I ever share my life again with a man
I would love to if I can
My life is different now and I'm ok with that
I find it hard with a man, even to chit chat
Well this is my life now and I have to deal with it
I'm sad today, or happy today, is something I can now admit

December

Winter is here and there's a chill in the air
Christmas is coming, so we don't really care
The leaves have blown all over the road
we brush them up, and put into a load
It's trying to rain and the sky is so grey
children are excited as they go out and play
We are all waiting and hoping for a drop of snow
out making snowballs, then watch out, as I throw
People decorate their homes and put up trees
santa will be coming soon, the kids shout with glee
Me, I haven't even started my shopping yet
I know what I'll buy, but I won't get myself into debt
Christmas will be different for me this year
it's getting near and I'm scared with fear
I'm not the person I was 12 months ago
I've had a heartbreaking year, yet I'm on the mend though
Christmas without George Michael, how will I cope
sometimes I think he wasn't stupid, smoking the dope
I wish I could go to bed, and sleep till new year
but would anyone know if I did just disappear